my
travel adventures

THIS BOOK BELONGS TO

....

only sleep once more

THE SHIP GOES THERE:

THEN STARTS OUR TRIP

THEN WE COME BACK

I REALLY WANT TO EXPERIENCE THAT:

I LOOK FORWARD TO THAT:

I DON'T WANT TO DO THAT:

This is how I imagine our cruise

I pack my suitcase and this comes with

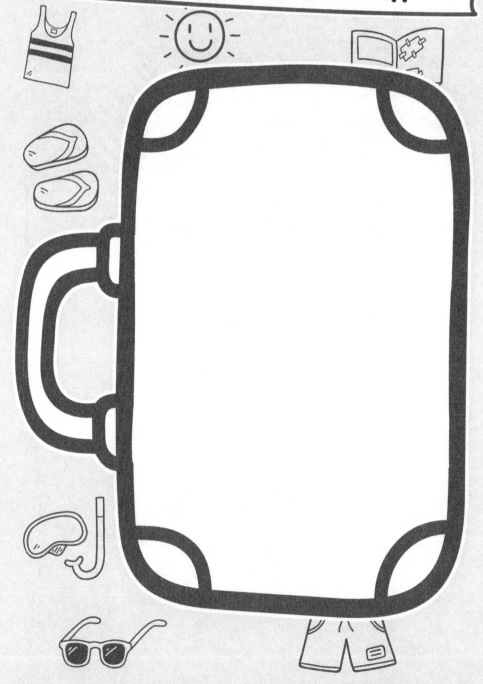

Finally we are off

We will travel with (please tick)

That's how many miles we travel (my parents say)

THAT'S HOW MANY HOURS WE WILL BE ON THE ROAD. (FOR EACH HOUR ONE POINT.)

AS LONG AS WE WERE REALLY ON THE WAY (MARKS FOR EACH HOUR A POINT.)

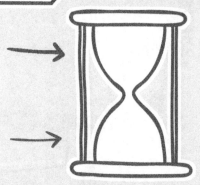

I'm so bored...

IF YOU ARE REALLY THAT BORED, THEN

WRITE DOWN ALL THE CITIES
THAT YOU WILL PASS:

. . . .

. . . .

. . . .

. . . .

. . . .

. . . .

THIS CITY HAD THE
FUNNIEST NAME

. . . .

COUNT IT:

CARS YOU HAVE PASSED . . . .

PEE BREAKS . . . .

TUNNEL . . . .

BRIDGES . . . .

PETROL STATIONS . . . .

ANIMALS . . . .

WITH THIS WE CAN PASS THE BOREDOM

☐ NAME, PLACE, ANIMAL, THING
☐ GUESS CAR LICENSE PLATE
☐ CAN YOU SEE WHAT I SEE
☐ GUESS ANIMAL SOUNDS

DRAW A PICTURE OF HOW IT LOOKS LIKE AT YOUR PLACE RIGHT NOW.

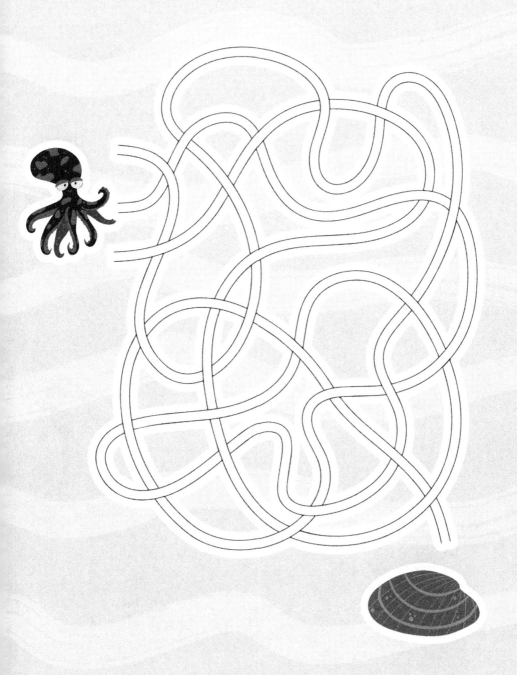

U	Y	A	S	V	D	S	E	Y	A
C	E	L	B	R	X	W	P	R	B
T	R	K	I	K	L	T	N	M	K
S	A	B	K	D	O	G	T	O	Q
J	B	R	M	T	B	F	J	N	N
X	B	P	H	S	L	C	R	K	R
R	I	Z	M	L	Z	N	B	E	O
P	T	X	H	D	G	Z	P	Y	I
G	I	R	W	P	C	A	T	Q	Z
W	K	G	B	O	Z	J	B	G	B

BIRD
DOG
RABBIT

CAT
MONKEY

```
U  L  U  M  Q  M  B  Y  Y  N
S  C  A  T  O  S  L  K  M  I
V  V  V  I  B  H  D  T  K  Y
C  K  K  Q  A  E  O  A  W  I
N  P  A  B  F  E  G  E  S  U
I  J  N  E  F  P  S  I  Q  Y
U  E  P  I  T  R  V  Z  P  V
N  C  Y  Z  O  R  S  M  V  N
N  I  D  H  L  X  X  X  Y  Z
D  M  A  R  A  B  B  I  T  K
```

CAT
HORSE
SHEEP

DOG
RABBIT

J	W	G	W	D	E	L	F	G	K
A	Z	R	C	J	H	G	O	O	E
V	A	C	A	T	I	O	N	J	J
C	Y	L	P	O	O	L	N	B	I
H	S	X	N	Z	J	U	Q	R	K
E	R	N	L	F	S	W	D	Z	G
Q	F	H	O	L	I	D	A	Y	T
Q	B	C	A	R	A	V	A	N	N
M	T	Z	K	S	P	L	H	O	L
U	I	T	Q	M	S	U	C	X	E

CARAVAN
POOL
VACATION

HOLIDAY
SUN

R	U	Z	V	K	B	T	D	U	E
C	W	E	H	B	J	W	Q	N	G
R	C	I	A	U	N	Z	O	N	X
S	K	P	D	C	M	T	I	W	S
C	M	R	T	K	S	W	R	H	Z
H	J	B	R	E	S	Q	T	Y	B
W	E	P	E	T	C	Y	N	B	C
J	Q	H	E	A	D	N	O	E	I
B	U	C	L	I	M	B	I	N	G
Z	W	H	D	X	H	H	O	T	I

BUCKET
STONE
TREE

CLIMBING
SWING

1

7	6					8	9	
	9		7	6				1
	1	8	4			5		
				7		2		4
7	1		2	9	4			
	4		3	1				8
			4	3	7			
9			6		1		5	3
5		6				1		

2

7							5	3
6			2			4		
		4		6	1			
			2	3	4			1
	9	8			7			
		5				3	6	7
	6			5			9	2
1		3	8			5		
9	8		4	7	2	1		

3

9	5	7		1				
						1	7	3
			6	8	7	9	2	
		3		5		2	6	
	2		9			5		
	1	5			8			
	6		7			3	9	
5			6			7		
1	7		9					4

4

7	4	1				2		
		9		5		1	3	8
			1	6	2			
6	9		7			5	4	
		4	6			9		5
5		7		1	4			
	7		3					1
			5	9		3		
	1	8					9	4

5

3	4	8	6		1			
		9	3	5	2			
						6	3	7
			2	3				
	9		8			1	7	3
	3	7			5		8	
4			9	1		2		8
2	7			6				4
9				3	4			

6

						8	6	4
	7	3			5			
1		4		2	9			7
				5			4	
	5		1		8	9	7	
9	4			3			1	5
			3	9	1			6
2	1	7						
	9		2			5		

7

	9				6		7	
	7					3	2	
	1		8			4		5
			1		8	7	6	2
7		1	6	2			5	4
		4	9					
5					9		4	7
			2	8				
2	3	9				5		1

8

6	7	5		1		9		
	9					1	2	3
			4	8				
7	3		9	4				
1			7			4	3	
4		2	5				1	
	1	3			7			2
2		7						1
		8			2		7	5

9

		6	4		1			
		5	9					2
		3			6	4	9	
1	8				5	7		
9	3		1			5	4	8
			2	4				1
7	2					8	5	
5		1		3		2		
3					7			

10

6	3			5				8
9					6	7		5
			9		7		1	6
				6		8		4
5	2	3				1		
			1	7	5	9		
	5	1				6	2	
		2		3	9		7	
		6	5		2			

11

			1			3		2
2	1	9			6	8		
4	6				7			
	2	1	6			4		
			7	3				9
		4	2			7	8	
3	7		6			2		8
8	4		5		3		1	
			8					5

12

5							8	
3				6	4	9		2
6	1			2	8	5	7	
		3	2				6	
	6	7	8			2		
		2	7			1	3	9
	8	6					5	
	3					7		4
			3	1	9	6		

13

		2	3			1		5
4	2			6	9	3		
9						6		4
			1	8			4	2
	8	1			5			
		6	3		2		8	
1						4		6
	7		8	5			3	
5	3		9	4				

14

6		3		2	4	7		
		8	1			5	6	2
4			9		7			8
				5	2			6
	4				1	8	5	
	1		6				4	
5		2		9			8	
8					6		7	5
		9	5					

15

		3			8	7		6
			9	6			3	1
7	4	6						9
	1			2	9			8
2	7				1		4	3
	8	4			5			
8						9		
9			1	7			4	3
				1		8	6	

16

	4		9	6			2	7
2		9			5			
		5			7			9
8	6			2			1	
	2		7	5			3	
5					1	3	8	4
				3		4	7	8
7		4						
9			4			2		3

17

4			1	3	6			
6				2	5			9
	5	3			1		4	2
5			6	4		7		
	4					3	2	5
1	8	2	9				6	4
					1	9		8
			6	7	3	2		
3	1	5						

18

	2	1	6	7				5
	5						1	9
	1					7		2
9		4			1		7	
6							8	
3			2	9				6
	4		2	7		5		
	7			1		6		4
	8	6	4				9	

19

```
. 2 8 | . 6 . | . . .
. . 7 | . 4 . | 5 6 .
. . . | . 1 7 | 8 4 .
------+-------+------
6 . 5 | . . 2 | . 7 .
8 . . | . . 6 | . 5 4
2 . . | 4 . 3 | . . .
------+-------+------
5 . . | 6 . . | 4 1 .
. . . | 5 . . | 9 . 8
. 8 3 | 7 . 4 | . . .
```

20

```
. 3 . | 7 . . | . . .
. . . | . 4 . | . . 8
9 4 . | . 2 8 | . 6 .
------+-------+------
. 6 . | 7 1 . | 5 . .
5 . . | 8 4 . | 6 7 .
4 8 . | 5 . . | 3 . 1
------+-------+------
7 1 3 | . . . | 4 . .
. . 4 | . . 6 | 9 3 .
. . 6 | 4 . . | 1 . .
```

21

```
. 2 4 | . . 9 | . . .
. . 6 | 3 . . | 1 8 .
. . 3 | . 7 6 | 5 . .
------+-------+------
. 7 . | 6 9 . | 4 3 1
4 5 . | . . . | 6 2 .
. . . | 8 2 4 | . . .
------+-------+------
. . . | 3 . . | . . 7
8 . . | 2 6 . | . . 9
9 . 2 | 4 . . | . . 6
```

22

```
. . . | 6 . . | 3 8 .
. . 3 | 9 1 . | 6 . .
6 . 7 | . 8 . | . . .
------+-------+------
4 2 . | 1 . . | 9 . .
. 1 . | 3 . 8 | . . 7
7 . . | . . . | 1 4 5
------+-------+------
1 . . | 4 . 2 | 7 . .
9 7 . | . . . | 5 2 1
3 . 2 | . . . | 9 4 .
```

23

```
7 . . | . 2 5 | . . .
. . 9 | . . 4 | 8 2 3
4 . 8 | . . . | . 1 .
------+-------+------
. . . | 1 3 6 | . . .
9 . 3 | 4 8 . | . 5 .
. 1 . | . 6 . | 4 . 7
------+-------+------
. 9 . | 7 . . | . . 1
1 7 . | 6 . 2 | . . 9
. . 2 | 9 . . | 3 . 6
```

24

```
9 3 2 | . . . | . . .
. 1 . | . 4 . | . 5 3
. 5 . | . 3 8 | . 7 .
------+-------+------
. . 1 | . . 2 | 9 8 4
. 9 . | 3 . . | . . 2
2 . . | 7 . 4 | . . .
------+-------+------
. . . | . 5 . | 4 . .
5 . . | 4 1 3 | 6 . .
7 . 6 | 8 . . | . 3 .
```

Our cruise ship

The name of our ship is:

· · · · · · · · · · · · · · · · · ·

There is room for that
many passengers:

· · · · · · · · · · · · · · · · · ·

The ship has that many decks:

· · · · · · · · · · · · · · · · · ·

Our cabin number:

· · · · · · · · · · · · · · · · · ·

○ INSIDE CABIN   ○ OUTSIDE CABIN   ○ BALCONY CABIN

That's where we're going with our cruise ship:

DATE: . . . .

WEATHER 🌡 . . . °F

THAT'S WHERE THE SHIP WAS TODAY:

📍 . . . .

THAT'S WHAT I EXPERIENCED TODAY:

. . . .

. . . .

. . . .

THAT'S WHAT I SAW TODAY:

. . . .

. . . .

. . . .

THIS IS WHAT I ATE TODAY:

. . . .

. . . .

. . . .

DRAW WHAT YOU HAVE EXPERIENCED TODAY:

OR INSERT PHOTOS, ENTRY CARDS OR STAMPS

MY FAVORITE MEMORY TODAY

. . . .

. . . .

I AM GRATEFUL FOR THAT TODAY

. . . .

. . . .

THIS IS HOW MY DAY WAS TODAY

DATE: . . . .

WEATHER 🌡 . . . °F

THAT'S WHERE THE SHIP WAS TODAY:

📍 . . . .

THAT'S WHAT I EXPERIENCED TODAY:

. . . .

. . . .

. . . .

THAT'S WHAT I SAW TODAY:

. . . .

. . . .

. . . .

THIS IS WHAT I ATE TODAY:

. . . .

. . . .

. . . .

DRAW WHAT YOU HAVE EXPERIENCED TODAY:

OR INSERT PHOTOS, ENTRY CARDS OR STAMPS

MY FAVORITE MEMORY TODAY

. . . .

. . . .

I AM GRATEFUL FOR THAT TODAY

. . . .

. . . .

THIS IS HOW MY DAY WAS TODAY

DATE: . . . .

THAT'S WHERE THE SHIP WAS TODAY:

📍 . . . .

WEATHER 🌡 . . . °F

THAT'S WHAT I EXPERIENCED TODAY:

. . . .

. . . .

. . . .

THAT'S WHAT I SAW TODAY:

. . . .

. . . .

. . . .

THIS IS WHAT I ATE TODAY:

. . . .

. . . .

. . . .

DRAW WHAT YOU HAVE EXPERIENCED TODAY:

OR INSERT PHOTOS, ENTRY CARDS OR STAMPS

MY FAVORITE MEMORY TODAY

. . . .

. . . .

I AM GRATEFUL FOR THAT TODAY

. . . .

. . . .

THIS IS HOW MY DAY WAS TODAY

DATE:

WEATHER 🌡 . . . °F

THAT'S WHERE THE SHIP WAS TODAY:

THAT'S WHAT I EXPERIENCED TODAY:

THAT'S WHAT I SAW TODAY:

THIS IS WHAT I ATE TODAY:

DRAW WHAT YOU HAVE EXPERIENCED TODAY:

OR INSERT PHOTOS, ENTRY CARDS OR STAMPS

MY FAVORITE MEMORY TODAY

. . . .

. . . .

I AM GRATEFUL FOR THAT TODAY

. . . .

. . . .

THIS IS HOW MY DAY WAS TODAY

DATE: . . . .

WEATHER 🌡 °F

THAT'S WHERE THE SHIP WAS TODAY:

THAT'S WHAT I EXPERIENCED TODAY:

. . . .

. . . .

. . . .

THAT'S WHAT I SAW TODAY:

. . . .

. . . .

. . . .

THIS IS WHAT I ATE TODAY:

. . . .

. . . .

. . . .

DRAW WHAT YOU HAVE EXPERIENCED TODAY:

OR INSERT PHOTOS, ENTRY CARDS OR STAMPS

MY FAVORITE MEMORY TODAY

. . . .

. . . .

I AM GRATEFUL FOR THAT TODAY

. . . .

. . . .

THIS IS HOW MY DAY WAS TODAY

DATE: . . . .

WEATHER 🌡 . . . °F

THAT'S WHERE THE SHIP WAS TODAY:

📍 . . . .

THAT'S WHAT I EXPERIENCED TODAY:

. . . .

. . . .

. . . .

THAT'S WHAT I SAW TODAY:

. . . .

. . . .

. . . .

THIS IS WHAT I ATE TODAY:

. . . .

. . . .

. . . .

DRAW WHAT YOU HAVE EXPERIENCED TODAY:

OR INSERT PHOTOS, ENTRY CARDS OR STAMPS

MY FAVORITE MEMORY TODAY

. . . .

. . . .

I AM GRATEFUL FOR THAT TODAY

. . . .

. . . .

THIS IS HOW MY DAY WAS TODAY

DATE: . . . .

WEATHER 🌡 . . . . °F

THAT'S WHERE THE SHIP WAS TODAY: . . . .

THAT'S WHAT I EXPERIENCED TODAY:

. . . .

. . . .

. . . .

THAT'S WHAT I SAW TODAY:

. . . .

. . . .

. . . .

THIS IS WHAT I ATE TODAY:

. . . .

. . . .

. . . .

DRAW WHAT YOU HAVE EXPERIENCED TODAY:

OR INSERT PHOTOS, ENTRY CARDS OR STAMPS

MY FAVORITE MEMORY TODAY

. . . .

. . . .

I AM GRATEFUL FOR THAT TODAY

. . . .

. . . .

THIS IS HOW MY DAY WAS TODAY

DATE: . . . .

WEATHER 🌡️ . . . . °F

THAT'S WHERE THE SHIP WAS TODAY:

📍 . . . .

THAT'S WHAT I EXPERIENCED TODAY:

. . . .

. . . .

. . . .

THAT'S WHAT I SAW TODAY:

. . . .

. . . .

. . . .

THIS IS WHAT I ATE TODAY:

. . . .

. . . .

. . . .

DRAW WHAT YOU HAVE EXPERIENCED TODAY:

OR INSERT PHOTOS, ENTRY CARDS OR STAMPS

MY FAVORITE MEMORY TODAY

. . . .

. . . .

I AM GRATEFUL FOR THAT TODAY

. . . .

. . . .

THIS IS HOW MY DAY WAS TODAY

DATE: . . . .

WEATHER 🌡 . . . °F

THAT'S WHERE THE SHIP WAS TODAY:

📍 . . . .
. . . .

THAT'S WHAT I EXPERIENCED TODAY:

. . . .

. . . .

. . . .

THAT'S WHAT I SAW TODAY:

. . . .

. . . .

. . . .

THIS IS WHAT I ATE TODAY:

. . . .

. . . .

. . . .

DRAW WHAT YOU HAVE EXPERIENCED TODAY:

OR INSERT PHOTOS, ENTRY CARDS OR STAMPS

MY FAVORITE MEMORY TODAY

. . . .

. . . .

I AM GRATEFUL FOR THAT TODAY

. . . .

. . . .

THIS IS HOW MY DAY WAS TODAY

DATE: . . . .

WEATHER 🌡 . . . °F

THAT'S WHERE THE SHIP WAS TODAY:

THAT'S WHAT I EXPERIENCED TODAY:

THAT'S WHAT I SAW TODAY:

THIS IS WHAT I ATE TODAY:

DRAW WHAT YOU HAVE EXPERIENCED TODAY:

OR INSERT PHOTOS, ENTRY CARDS OR STAMPS

MY FAVORITE MEMORY TODAY

. . . .

. . . .

I AM GRATEFUL FOR THAT TODAY

. . . .

. . . .

THIS IS HOW MY DAY WAS TODAY

DATE: . . . .

WEATHER 🌡 . . . °F

THAT'S WHERE THE SHIP WAS TODAY:

📍 . . . .
. . . .

THAT'S WHAT I EXPERIENCED TODAY:

. . . .

. . . .

. . . .

THAT'S WHAT I SAW TODAY:

. . . .

. . . .

. . . .

THIS IS WHAT I ATE TODAY:

. . . .

. . . .

. . . .

DRAW WHAT YOU HAVE EXPERIENCED TODAY:

OR INSERT PHOTOS, ENTRY CARDS OR STAMPS

MY FAVORITE MEMORY TODAY

. . . .

. . . .

I AM GRATEFUL FOR THAT TODAY

. . . .

. . . .

THIS IS HOW MY DAY WAS TODAY

DATE: . . . .

WEATHER 🌡 . . . . °F

THAT'S WHERE THE SHIP WAS TODAY:

📍 . . . .

THAT'S WHAT I EXPERIENCED TODAY:

. . . .

. . . .

. . . .

THAT'S WHAT I SAW TODAY:

. . . .

. . . .

. . . .

THIS IS WHAT I ATE TODAY:

. . . .

. . . .

. . . .

DRAW WHAT YOU HAVE EXPERIENCED TODAY:

OR INSERT PHOTOS, ENTRY CARDS OR STAMPS

MY FAVORITE MEMORY TODAY

. . . .

. . . .

I AM GRATEFUL FOR THAT TODAY

. . . .

. . . .

THIS IS HOW MY DAY WAS TODAY

DATE: . . . .

THAT'S WHERE THE SHIP WAS TODAY:

. . . .

WEATHER . . . . °F

THAT'S WHAT I EXPERIENCED TODAY:

. . . .

. . . .

. . . .

THAT'S WHAT I SAW TODAY:

. . . .

. . . .

. . . .

THIS IS WHAT I ATE TODAY:

. . . .

. . . .

. . . .

DRAW WHAT YOU HAVE EXPERIENCED TODAY:

OR INSERT PHOTOS, ENTRY CARDS OR STAMPS

MY FAVORITE MEMORY TODAY

. . . .

. . . .

I AM GRATEFUL FOR THAT TODAY

. . . .

. . . .

THIS IS HOW MY DAY WAS TODAY

DATE: . . . .

THAT'S WHERE THE SHIP WAS TODAY:

. . . .

WEATHER 🌡 . . . . °F

THAT'S WHAT I EXPERIENCED TODAY:

. . . .

. . . .

. . . .

THAT'S WHAT I SAW TODAY:

. . . .

. . . .

. . . .

THIS IS WHAT I ATE TODAY:

. . . .

. . . .

. . . .

DRAW WHAT YOU HAVE EXPERIENCED TODAY:

OR INSERT PHOTOS, ENTRY CARDS OR STAMPS

MY FAVORITE MEMORY TODAY

. . . .

. . . .

I AM GRATEFUL FOR THAT TODAY

. . . .

. . . .

THIS IS HOW MY DAY WAS TODAY

DATE: . . . .

THAT'S WHERE THE SHIP WAS TODAY:

WEATHER 🌡 . . . . °F

THAT'S WHAT I EXPERIENCED TODAY:

. . . .

. . . .

. . . .

THAT'S WHAT I SAW TODAY:

. . . .

. . . .

. . . .

THIS IS WHAT I ATE TODAY:

. . . .

. . . .

. . . .

DRAW WHAT YOU HAVE EXPERIENCED TODAY:

OR INSERT PHOTOS, ENTRY CARDS OR STAMPS

MY FAVORITE MEMORY TODAY

. . . .

. . . .

I AM GRATEFUL FOR THAT TODAY

. . . .

. . . .

THIS IS HOW MY DAY WAS TODAY

DATE: . . . .

WEATHER 🌡 . . . °F

THAT'S WHERE THE SHIP WAS TODAY:
. . . .

THAT'S WHAT I EXPERIENCED TODAY:

. . . .

. . . .

. . . .

THAT'S WHAT I SAW TODAY:

. . . .

. . . .

. . . .

THIS IS WHAT I ATE TODAY:

. . . .

. . . .

. . . .

DRAW WHAT YOU HAVE EXPERIENCED TODAY:

OR INSERT PHOTOS, ENTRY CARDS OR STAMPS

MY FAVORITE MEMORY TODAY

. . . .

. . . .

I AM GRATEFUL FOR THAT TODAY

. . . .

. . . .

THIS IS HOW MY DAY WAS TODAY

DATE: . . . .

WEATHER 🌡 . . . . °F

THAT'S WHERE THE SHIP WAS TODAY:

📍 . . . .

THAT'S WHAT I EXPERIENCED TODAY:

. . . .

. . . .

. . . .

THAT'S WHAT I SAW TODAY:

. . . .

. . . .

. . . .

THIS IS WHAT I ATE TODAY:

. . . .

. . . .

. . . .

DRAW WHAT YOU HAVE EXPERIENCED TODAY:

OR INSERT PHOTOS, ENTRY CARDS OR STAMPS

MY FAVORITE MEMORY TODAY

. . . .

. . . .

I AM GRATEFUL FOR THAT TODAY

. . . .

. . . .

THIS IS HOW MY DAY WAS TODAY

DATE: . . . .

WEATHER 🌡 . . . °F

THAT'S WHERE THE SHIP WAS TODAY:

📍 . . . .

THAT'S WHAT I EXPERIENCED TODAY:

. . . .

. . . .

. . . .

THAT'S WHAT I SAW TODAY:

. . . .

. . . .

. . . .

THIS IS WHAT I ATE TODAY:

. . . .

. . . .

. . . .

DRAW WHAT YOU HAVE EXPERIENCED TODAY:

OR INSERT PHOTOS, ENTRY CARDS OR STAMPS

MY FAVORITE MEMORY TODAY

. . . .

. . . .

I AM GRATEFUL FOR THAT TODAY

. . . .

. . . .

THIS IS HOW MY DAY WAS TODAY

DATE: . . . .

WEATHER 🌡 . . . °F

THAT'S WHERE THE SHIP WAS TODAY:

📍 . . . .
. . . .

THAT'S WHAT I EXPERIENCED TODAY:

. . . .

. . . .

. . . .

THAT'S WHAT I SAW TODAY:

. . . .

. . . .

. . . .

THIS IS WHAT I ATE TODAY:

. . . .

. . . .

. . . .

DRAW WHAT YOU HAVE EXPERIENCED TODAY:

OR INSERT PHOTOS, ENTRY CARDS OR STAMPS

MY FAVORITE MEMORY TODAY

. . . .

. . . .

I AM GRATEFUL FOR THAT TODAY

. . . .

. . . .

THIS IS HOW MY DAY WAS TODAY

DATE: . . . .

WEATHER 🌡 . . . °F

THAT'S WHERE THE SHIP WAS TODAY:
📍 . . . .

THAT'S WHAT I EXPERIENCED TODAY:

. . . .

. . . .

. . . .

THAT'S WHAT I SAW TODAY:

. . . .

. . . .

. . . .

THIS IS WHAT I ATE TODAY:

. . . .

. . . .

. . . .

DRAW WHAT YOU HAVE EXPERIENCED TODAY:

OR INSERT PHOTOS, ENTRY CARDS OR STAMPS

MY FAVORITE MEMORY TODAY

. . . .

. . . .

I AM GRATEFUL FOR THAT TODAY

. . . .

. . . .

THIS IS HOW MY DAY WAS TODAY

DATE: . . . .

WEATHER 🌡 . . . °F

THAT'S WHERE THE SHIP WAS TODAY:

📍 . . . .
. . . .

THAT'S WHAT I EXPERIENCED TODAY:

. . . .

. . . .

. . . .

THAT'S WHAT I SAW TODAY:

. . . .

. . . .

. . . .

THIS IS WHAT I ATE TODAY:

. . . .

. . . .

. . . .

DRAW WHAT YOU HAVE EXPERIENCED TODAY:

OR INSERT PHOTOS, ENTRY CARDS OR STAMPS

MY FAVORITE MEMORY TODAY

. . . .

. . . .

I AM GRATEFUL FOR THAT TODAY

. . . .

. . . .

THIS IS HOW MY DAY WAS TODAY

DATE: . . . .

WEATHER 🌡 . . . °F

THAT'S WHERE THE SHIP WAS TODAY:

📍 . . . .

THAT'S WHAT I EXPERIENCED TODAY:

. . . .

. . . .

. . . .

THAT'S WHAT I SAW TODAY:

. . . .

. . . .

. . . .

THIS IS WHAT I ATE TODAY:

. . . .

. . . .

. . . .

DRAW WHAT YOU HAVE EXPERIENCED TODAY:

OR INSERT PHOTOS, ENTRY CARDS OR STAMPS

MY FAVORITE MEMORY TODAY

. . . .

. . . .

I AM GRATEFUL FOR THAT TODAY

. . . .

. . . .

THIS IS HOW MY DAY WAS TODAY

DATE: . . . .

WEATHER 🌡 . . . . °F

THAT'S WHERE THE SHIP WAS TODAY:

📍 . . . .

. . . .

THAT'S WHAT I EXPERIENCED TODAY:

. . . .

. . . .

. . . .

THAT'S WHAT I SAW TODAY:

. . . .

. . . .

THIS IS WHAT I ATE TODAY:

. . . .

. . . .

. . . .

DRAW WHAT YOU HAVE EXPERIENCED TODAY:

OR INSERT PHOTOS, ENTRY CARDS OR STAMPS

MY FAVORITE MEMORY TODAY

. . . .

I AM GRATEFUL FOR THAT TODAY

. . . .

. . . .

THIS IS HOW MY DAY WAS TODAY

DATE: . . . .

WEATHER 🌡 . . . °F

THAT'S WHERE THE SHIP WAS TODAY:

📍 . . . .

THAT'S WHAT I EXPERIENCED TODAY:

. . . .

. . . .

. . . .

THAT'S WHAT I SAW TODAY:

. . . .

. . . .

. . . .

THIS IS WHAT I ATE TODAY:

. . . .

. . . .

. . . .

DRAW WHAT YOU HAVE EXPERIENCED TODAY:

OR INSERT PHOTOS, ENTRY CARDS OR STAMPS

MY FAVORITE MEMORY TODAY

. . . .

. . . .

I AM GRATEFUL FOR THAT TODAY

. . . .

. . . .

THIS IS HOW MY DAY WAS TODAY

DATE: . . . .

WEATHER 🌡 . . . °F

THAT'S WHERE THE SHIP WAS TODAY:

📍 . . . .

. . . .

THAT'S WHAT I EXPERIENCED TODAY:

. . . .

. . . .

. . . .

THAT'S WHAT I SAW TODAY:

. . . .

. . . .

. . . .

THIS IS WHAT I ATE TODAY:

. . . .

. . . .

. . . .

DRAW WHAT YOU HAVE EXPERIENCED TODAY:

OR INSERT PHOTOS, ENTRY CARDS OR STAMPS

MY FAVORITE MEMORY TODAY

. . . .

. . . .

I AM GRATEFUL FOR THAT TODAY

. . . .

. . . .

THIS IS HOW MY DAY WAS TODAY

DATE: . . . .

WEATHER 🌡 . . . . °F

THAT'S WHERE THE SHIP WAS TODAY: . . . .

THAT'S WHAT I EXPERIENCED TODAY:

. . . .

. . . .

. . . .

THAT'S WHAT I SAW TODAY:

. . . .

. . . .

. . . .

THIS IS WHAT I ATE TODAY:

. . . .

. . . .

. . . .

DRAW WHAT YOU HAVE EXPERIENCED TODAY:

OR INSERT PHOTOS, ENTRY CARDS OR STAMPS

MY FAVORITE MEMORY TODAY

. . . .

. . . .

I AM GRATEFUL FOR THAT TODAY

. . . .

. . . .

THIS IS HOW MY DAY WAS TODAY

DATE: . . . .

WEATHER 🌡 . . . °F

THAT'S WHERE THE SHIP WAS TODAY:

THAT'S WHAT I EXPERIENCED TODAY:

THAT'S WHAT I SAW TODAY:

THIS IS WHAT I ATE TODAY:

DRAW WHAT YOU HAVE EXPERIENCED TODAY:

OR INSERT PHOTOS, ENTRY CARDS OR STAMPS

MY FAVORITE MEMORY TODAY

· ·

· ·

I AM GRATEFUL FOR THAT TODAY

· ·

· ·

THIS IS HOW MY DAY WAS TODAY

DATE: . . . .

THAT'S WHERE THE SHIP WAS TODAY:

📍 . . . .

WEATHER 🌡 . . . °F

THAT'S WHAT I EXPERIENCED TODAY:

. . . .

. . . .

. . . .

THAT'S WHAT I SAW TODAY:

. . . .

. . . .

. . . .

THIS IS WHAT I ATE TODAY:

. . . .

. . . .

. . . .

DRAW WHAT YOU HAVE EXPERIENCED TODAY:

OR INSERT PHOTOS, ENTRY CARDS OR STAMPS

MY FAVORITE MEMORY TODAY

. . . .

. . . .

I AM GRATEFUL FOR THAT TODAY

. . . .

. . . .

THIS IS HOW MY DAY WAS TODAY

DATE: . . . .

WEATHER 🌡 . . . . °F

THAT'S WHERE THE SHIP WAS TODAY:

📍 . . . .

THAT'S WHAT I EXPERIENCED TODAY:

. . . .

. . . .

. . . .

THAT'S WHAT I SAW TODAY:

. . . .

. . . .

. . . .

THIS IS WHAT I ATE TODAY:

. . . .

. . . .

. . . .

DRAW WHAT YOU HAVE EXPERIENCED TODAY:

OR INSERT PHOTOS, ENTRY CARDS OR STAMPS

MY FAVORITE MEMORY TODAY

. . . .

. . . .

I AM GRATEFUL FOR THAT TODAY

. . . .

. . . .

THIS IS HOW MY DAY WAS TODAY

DATE: . . . .

WEATHER 🌡 . . . °F

THAT'S WHERE THE SHIP WAS TODAY:

📍 . . . .

THAT'S WHAT I EXPERIENCED TODAY:

. . . .

. . . .

. . . .

THAT'S WHAT I SAW TODAY:

. . . .

. . . .

. . . .

THIS IS WHAT I ATE TODAY:

. . . .

. . . .

. . . .

DRAW WHAT YOU HAVE EXPERIENCED TODAY:

OR INSERT PHOTOS, ENTRY CARDS OR STAMPS

MY FAVORITE MEMORY TODAY

. . . .

. . . .

I AM GRATEFUL FOR THAT TODAY

. . . .

. . . .

THIS IS HOW MY DAY WAS TODAY

DATE: . . . .

WEATHER 🌡️ . . . . °F

THAT'S WHERE THE SHIP WAS TODAY:

📍 . . . .

. . . .

THAT'S WHAT I EXPERIENCED TODAY:

. . . .

. . . .

. . . .

THAT'S WHAT I SAW TODAY:

. . . .

. . . .

. . . .

THIS IS WHAT I ATE TODAY:

. . . .

. . . .

. . . .

DRAW WHAT YOU HAVE EXPERIENCED TODAY:

OR INSERT PHOTOS, ENTRY CARDS OR STAMPS

MY FAVORITE MEMORY TODAY

. . . .

. . . .

I AM GRATEFUL FOR THAT TODAY

. . . .

. . . .

THIS IS HOW MY DAY WAS TODAY

DATE: . . . .

WEATHER 🌡 . . . **°F**

THAT'S WHERE THE SHIP WAS TODAY:

📍 . . . .

THAT'S WHAT I EXPERIENCED TODAY:

. . . .

. . . .

. . . .

THAT'S WHAT I SAW TODAY:

. . . .

. . . .

. . . .

THIS IS WHAT I ATE TODAY:

. . . .

. . . .

. . . .

DRAW WHAT YOU HAVE EXPERIENCED TODAY:

OR INSERT PHOTOS, ENTRY CARDS OR STAMPS

MY FAVORITE MEMORY TODAY

. . . .

. . . .

I AM GRATEFUL FOR THAT TODAY

. . . .

. . . .

THIS IS HOW MY DAY WAS TODAY

DATE: . . . .

WEATHER 🌡 . . . °F

THAT'S WHERE THE
SHIP WAS TODAY:
📍 . . . .
. . . .

THAT'S WHAT I EXPERIENCED TODAY:

. . . .

. . . .

. . . .

THAT'S WHAT I SAW TODAY:

. . . .

. . . .

. . . .

THIS IS WHAT I ATE TODAY:

. . . .

. . . .

. . . .

DRAW WHAT YOU HAVE EXPERIENCED TODAY:

OR INSERT PHOTOS, ENTRY CARDS OR STAMPS

MY FAVORITE MEMORY TODAY

. . . .

. . . .

I AM GRATEFUL FOR THAT TODAY

. . . .

. . . .

THIS IS HOW MY DAY WAS TODAY

DATE: . . . .

WEATHER 🌡 . . . °F

THAT'S WHERE THE SHIP WAS TODAY:

📍 . . . .

THAT'S WHAT I EXPERIENCED TODAY:

. . . .

. . . .

. . . .

THAT'S WHAT I SAW TODAY:

. . . .

. . . .

. . . .

THIS IS WHAT I ATE TODAY:

. . . .

. . . .

. . . .

DRAW WHAT YOU HAVE EXPERIENCED TODAY:

OR INSERT PHOTOS, ENTRY CARDS OR STAMPS

MY FAVORITE MEMORY TODAY

. . . .

. . . .

I AM GRATEFUL FOR THAT TODAY

. . . .

. . . .

THIS IS HOW MY DAY WAS TODAY

DATE: . . . .

THAT'S WHERE THE SHIP WAS TODAY:

WEATHER . . . **°F**

THAT'S WHAT I EXPERIENCED TODAY:

THAT'S WHAT I SAW TODAY:

THIS IS WHAT I ATE TODAY:

DRAW WHAT YOU HAVE EXPERIENCED TODAY:

OR INSERT PHOTOS, ENTRY CARDS OR STAMPS

MY FAVORITE MEMORY TODAY

. . . .

. . . .

I AM GRATEFUL FOR THAT TODAY

. . . .

. . . .

THIS IS HOW MY DAY WAS TODAY

DATE: . . . .

WEATHER 🌡 . . . °F

THAT'S WHERE THE SHIP WAS TODAY:

📍 . . . .

THAT'S WHAT I EXPERIENCED TODAY:

. . . .

. . . .

. . . .

THAT'S WHAT I SAW TODAY:

. . . .

. . . .

. . . .

THIS IS WHAT I ATE TODAY:

. . . .

. . . .

. . . .

DRAW WHAT YOU HAVE EXPERIENCED TODAY:

OR INSERT PHOTOS, ENTRY CARDS OR STAMPS

MY FAVORITE MEMORY TODAY

. . . .

. . . .

I AM GRATEFUL FOR THAT TODAY

. . . .

. . . .

THIS IS HOW MY DAY WAS TODAY

DATE: . . . .

WEATHER 🌡 . . . . °F

THAT'S WHERE THE SHIP WAS TODAY:

📍 . . . .
. . . .

THAT'S WHAT I EXPERIENCED TODAY:

. . . .

. . . .

. . . .

THAT'S WHAT I SAW TODAY:

. . . .

. . . .

. . . .

THIS IS WHAT I ATE TODAY:

. . . .

. . . .

. . . .

DRAW WHAT YOU HAVE EXPERIENCED TODAY:

OR INSERT PHOTOS, ENTRY CARDS OR STAMPS

MY FAVORITE MEMORY TODAY

. . . .

. . . .

I AM GRATEFUL FOR THAT TODAY

. . . .

. . . .

THIS IS HOW MY DAY WAS TODAY

DATE: . . . .

WEATHER 🌡 . . . °F

THAT'S WHERE THE
SHIP WAS TODAY:

📍 . . . .

THAT'S WHAT I EXPERIENCED TODAY:

. . . .

. . . .

. . . .

THAT'S WHAT I SAW TODAY:

. . . .

. . . .

. . . .

THIS IS WHAT I ATE TODAY:

. . . .

. . . .

. . . .

DRAW WHAT YOU HAVE EXPERIENCED TODAY:

OR INSERT PHOTOS, ENTRY CARDS OR STAMPS

MY FAVORITE MEMORY TODAY

. . . .

. . . .

I AM GRATEFUL FOR THAT TODAY

. . . .

. . . .

THIS IS HOW MY DAY WAS TODAY

DATE: . . . .

WEATHER 🌡 . . . . °F

THAT'S WHERE THE SHIP WAS TODAY:

. . . .

. . . .

THAT'S WHAT I EXPERIENCED TODAY:

. . . .

. . . .

. . . .

THAT'S WHAT I SAW TODAY:

. . . .

. . . .

. . . .

THIS IS WHAT I ATE TODAY:

. . . .

. . . .

. . . .

DRAW WHAT YOU HAVE EXPERIENCED TODAY:

OR INSERT PHOTOS, ENTRY CARDS OR STAMPS

MY FAVORITE MEMORY TODAY

· ·

· ·

I AM GRATEFUL FOR THAT TODAY

· ·

· ·

THIS IS HOW MY DAY WAS TODAY

DATE: . . . .

WEATHER 🌡 . . . . . . °F

THAT'S WHERE THE SHIP WAS TODAY: . . . .

THAT'S WHAT I EXPERIENCED TODAY:

. . . .

. . . .

. . . .

THAT'S WHAT I SAW TODAY:

. . . .

. . . .

. . . .

THIS IS WHAT I ATE TODAY:

. . . .

. . . .

. . . .

DRAW WHAT YOU HAVE EXPERIENCED TODAY:

OR INSERT PHOTOS, ENTRY CARDS OR STAMPS

MY FAVORITE MEMORY TODAY

. . . .

. . . .

I AM GRATEFUL FOR THAT TODAY

. . . .

. . . .

THIS IS HOW MY DAY WAS TODAY

DATE: . . . .

WEATHER 🌡 . . . °F

THAT'S WHERE THE SHIP WAS TODAY:
. . . .
. . . .

THAT'S WHAT I EXPERIENCED TODAY:

. . . .

. . . .

. . . .

THAT'S WHAT I SAW TODAY:

. . . .

. . . .

. . . .

THIS IS WHAT I ATE TODAY:

. . . .

. . . .

. . . .

DRAW WHAT YOU HAVE EXPERIENCED TODAY:

OR INSERT PHOTOS, ENTRY CARDS OR STAMPS

MY FAVORITE MEMORY TODAY

....

....

I AM GRATEFUL FOR THAT TODAY

....

....

THIS IS HOW MY DAY WAS TODAY

NEW FRIENDS
I MET ON THE CRUISE

FIRST NAME   NAME   STREET

CITY   EMAIL   PHONENUMBER

FIRST NAME   NAME   STREET

CITY   EMAIL   PHONENUMBER

FIRST NAME   NAME   STREET

CITY   EMAIL   PHONENUMBER

NEW FRIENDS
I MET ON THE CRUISE

FIRST NAME   NAME   STREET

. . . .

CITY   EMAIL   PHONENUMBER

. . . .

FIRST NAME   NAME   STREET

. . . .

CITY   EMAIL   PHONENUMBER

. . . .

FIRST NAME   NAME   STREET

. . . .

CITY   EMAIL   PHONENUMBER

. . . .

NEW FRIENDS
I MET ON THE CRUISE

FIRST NAME   NAME   STREET

. . . .

CITY   EMAIL   PHONENUMBER

. . . .

FIRST NAME   NAME   STREET

. . . .

CITY   EMAIL   PHONENUMBER

. . . .

FIRST NAME   NAME   STREET

. . . .

CITY   EMAIL   PHONENUMBER

. . . .

NEW FRIENDS
I MET ON THE CRUISE

FIRST NAME   NAME   STREET

· ·

CITY   EMAIL   PHONENUMBER

· ·

FIRST NAME   NAME   STREET

· ·

CITY   EMAIL   PHONENUMBER

· ·

FIRST NAME   NAME   STREET

· ·

CITY   EMAIL   PHONENUMBER

· ·

NEW FRIENDS
I MET ON THE CRUISE

FIRST NAME   NAME   STREET

. . . .

CITY   EMAIL   PHONENUMBER

. . . .

FIRST NAME   NAME   STREET

. . . .

CITY   EMAIL   PHONENUMBER

. . . .

FIRST NAME   NAME   STREET

. . . .

CITY   EMAIL   PHONENUMBER

. . . .

NEW FRIENDS
I MET ON THE CRUISE

FIRST NAME   NAME   STREET

CITY   EMAIL   PHONENUMBER

FIRST NAME   NAME   STREET

CITY   EMAIL   PHONENUMBER

FIRST NAME   NAME   STREET

CITY   EMAIL   PHONENUMBER

WE WOULD LiKE TO OFFER OUR PRODUCTS TO
OUR CUSTOMERS
CONSTANTLY iMPROVE.

WiTH FEEDBACK iN THE FORM OF A
REVIEW, WE CAN ALSO SHARE THEIR
POSiTiVE EXPERiENCES, PRAiSE AND
CRITICISM CAN BE TAKEN iNTO ACCOUNT.

Contact
Björn Meyer
Rönnehof 5
30457 Hannover, Germany
Override2000@gmx.de
Cover design: Björn Meyer
Design elements: vecteezy.com
www.creativefabrica.com